Pete Maravich, Basketball Magician

by LOU SABIN

SCHOLASTIC BOOK SERVICES

NEW YORK · TORONTO · LONDON · AUCKLAND · SYDNEY · TOKYO

For Fran and Keith, my best friends

Copyright © 1973 by Louis Sabin. All rights reserved. Published by Scholastic Book Services, a division of Scholastic Magazines, Inc.

1st printing.....................January 1973

Printed in the U.S.A.

CONTENTS

Rookie Under Fire   5

A Star Is Born   10

Basketball's Wonder Child   17

Father and Son   26

"The Fastest Gun in the South"   31

The All-Star Freshman   41

Pete Rewrites the Record Books   48

The Star Is Dimmed   58

"I'd Rather Shoot Than Switch"   73

Last-Second Heroics   77

The All-Time Scoring Champion   88

The Pistol Enters the Pros   98

NBA Rookie   104

A Real Pro   114

Pete's Future   125

"Pistol Pete" Maravich

Rookie Under Fire

AT THE REFEREE'S WHISTLE, the ball is tossed for the center jump. Seconds later Pete Maravich is dribbling from the Atlanta Hawks' backcourt toward the waiting New York Knickerbockers. The Hawk rookie moves smoothly, the ball bouncing from his right hand to the floor and back, as if ball and hand were connected by an invisible string.

For the 19,500 fans watching, the exciting play of Pete Maravich is one of the reasons they have jammed New York's Madison Square Garden on this November night in 1970. They want to see, with their own eyes, if "Pistol Pete" will dip into his famous bag of tricks and outwit the champions of the NBA (National Basketball Association).

5

Walt Hazzard, Pete's backcourt partner, moves deeper into Knick territory for a pass from Pete. But instead of passing, Maravich continues to dribble.

He shifts the ball from right hand to left and weaves past Walt Frazier, the Knick guarding him. Now Pete turns on a burst of speed; the ball is a blur beside his flying feet. Suddenly two New York defenders — Dick Barnett and Bill Bradley — are between him and the basket.

Maravich skids to a stop. A swift glance at the clock tells him he has just a few seconds left. If one of the Hawk players doesn't take a shot within 24 seconds from when the Hawks got the ball, the Knicks will take possession.

Maravich must either pass or shoot it himself. He looks around for a teammate to throw to, but finds them all closely guarded. In desperation he leaps and flings the ball at the net. It bangs off the rim of the basket, and New York's Willis Reed grabs the rebound.

As Pete hurries back on defense, he hears a voice from the stands call out, "Cut out the fancy stuff, Maravich! You're playing in the pros now!"

There is no sign that Maravich has heard the fan as he trots downcourt. His job now is to stop Walt Frazier from scoring or setting up one of the other Knicks for a shot.

But Frazier shows Pete the way he became an All-Pro in the world's toughest league. While Maravich plays him closely, Frazier watches Willis Reed, the Knick center, work closer to the Hawk basket. When Frazier fakes a pass to Reed, Pete moves to stop it, and Walt flips the ball to Bradley instead.

Maravich follows the flight of the ball, taking his eyes off Frazier for just an instant. That's all the New York guard needs. He is past Maravich, speeding toward the basket. The return pass from Bradley slaps into his hands, and he drives in for an easy layup.

It is mistake number two for Maravich. Again a voice from the crowd calls out, "Hey, Pistol Pete, wake up! They're not firing blanks out there!"

The Atlanta coach, Richie Guerin, calls time out. His players huddle around him, listening to his instructions. When the Hawks run back on the court, Pete Maravich isn't among them. He is on the bench, and Jerry Chambers is in his place in the Atlanta lineup.

The Knick fans clap with pleasure. It is clear they feel their Walt Frazier has put the highly praised newcomer in his place. The New York fans are here to see if Maravich can really play the great basketball they've read about. But they are also hoping to see the college wonder boy shown up by their team. And so they are very happy. The Knicks are off to a fast lead and have already put Atlanta's sensation on the sideline.

Maravich doesn't stay on the bench long. After some advice and encouragement from Coach Guerin, he is sent back in. The crowd leans forward to see what Maravich will do next. Will he improve? Or will Frazier continue to pin him down?

Atlanta's players move into the Knick forecourt. Hazzard brings the ball past the midcourt line, ducks to his left, and sends a sharp pass to Maravich.

Pete starts to cut toward the hoop only to find Frazier blocking his path. Still dribbling, he darts toward the right-hand corner, his eyes glued to the basket. Everyone in the arena is certain he is after only one thing: two points for Pete Maravich. His teammates get into position to grab the rebound if Maravich misses.

Just at this moment Maravich catches everyone by surprise. He speeds his dribble and takes a fast step toward the basket. But instead of shooting, he whips a behind-the-back pass to forward Lou Hudson. Only Hudson isn't there any more. He had broken for the basket to be in rebound position. The ball slaps against the floor and skips into the hands of Dick Barnett.

A cascade of jeers and laughter spills out of the stands. Maravich has done it again — mistake number three, and the Knicks have the ball.

Before the game is over, Pete Maravich commits a total of seven such mistakes. Each one causes Atlanta to lose possession of the ball. Seven times his team misses an opportunity to score. Seven times the Knicks do get to shoot.

In the losers' dressing room, a silent Pete Maravich sits in front of his locker. His shoulders are slumped and his eyes remain fixed on his shoelaces. Making simple mistakes and looking foolish have not been part of this young man's career. Until this season he has known only cheers and success. But now it seems as if all those years of basketball and the countless hours of practice have been wasted.

At this moment, he knows, the fans are wondering about his future as a pro. Will the college hero learn to mesh his immense talents with those of his Hawk teammates? Or will he be just another glamorous rookie who couldn't make it in the NBA?

Sitting there in the heavy silence, Pete Maravich is at a crossroads in his career.

A Star Is Born

THE STORY OF PETE PRESS MARAVICH began in Sewickley, Pennsylvania, a small town near Pittsburgh, where he was born on June 22, 1948.

Right from the start, Pete's life was surrounded by the idea of winning and losing. And even in those first few years, although he couldn't understand anything about the game, Pete sensed that basketball was important. It paid for his family's food, clothing, the house they lived in — everything — because his father, Press Maravich, was a professional basketball player, a hustling guard with the Pittsburgh Ironmen and the Youngstown Bears of the Basketball Association of America.

Pete was his father's son from the day he was born. He was quiet and obedient, especially to the hero-father he idolized. Press Maravich, recalling the tiny, blond-haired boy for whom he already had great dreams, said, "He was the best kid. Why, we'd put him in a stroller when he was a year old, and he wouldn't budge." And Pete's mother remembers that, as a toddler, her little boy "carried a basketball while other kids carried teddy bears."

Whenever Pete cuddled his basketball, he saw his Dad smile approvingly, so the child quickly recognized that this was a way of pleasing his hero. To Pete's father, it meant that Pete had already chosen his future.

Pete doesn't remember much about those preschool years. What he does remember is the Christmas Day he received his very own ball as a gift from his father. He said, "I first started playing around with a basketball when I was seven." But, he continued, "it was just a toy. Like my bicycle and fire engines and toy guns." His father didn't think of the basketball as a toy, though, and soon neither did young Pete.

The Maravich family — Pete; his mother; father; and half brother Ronnie, who was three years older — moved from Pennsylvania to South

Carolina. His father had retired from playing professional basketball, a job that had kept him away from home much of the time. Now he was coaching the team at Clemson University in South Carolina.

With Press at home, father and son had many more hours and days to be together and to build their unique basketball relationship. If Pete had played more with other kids instead of spending all of his free time practicing basketball with his father, he might have grown up as more of a team person than a loner. But developing his skill with a basketball was what meant most to young Pete, and that meant rushing home after school to his father.

"I'd see Pete coming in the yard," said Press, "and I'd run for the basketball and start shooting. Wherever we lived, I always had a basket in the back yard."

"From the time I was seven until I was 15," Pete said, "I played basketball just about all year — nine, 10 hours every day."

Everywhere he went, the round ball was his constant companion. He would walk two miles from his house to the town of Clemson, dribbling the ball all the way. And when he reached town, he would head for the YMCA where a basket waited for him. Pete was now looking for competition. If there were other boys in the gym, he would sharpen his skills against real players. If no other boys were around, he would create game situations in his mind and go man-to-man against phantom guards, forwards, and centers. There was always play-by-play action in the court of his imagination.

At home, at the "Y" — even at the movies — Pete practiced. "I'd be sure to take my ball with me," he said, "and be sure to get an end seat. That way I could dribble in the aisle while the movies were on." The other theater-goers didn't complain; they were probably delighted by the "live" show.

Back home, in the yard, Pete and Press worked on all the important things a player must learn if he wants to keep improving his game. One day it would be shooting. Another day, dribbling. Another day, passing. Different plays, different moves. Getting the "feel" of the ball in all situations. The only thing that may have been neglected was defense. The focus was all on Pete's becoming the perfect shooter, the offensive point-maker. That's what catches the eye of scouts, and what delights fans the most.

By the time Pete was 11, he was growing slightly bored with doing just "ordinary" things with a basketball. So, when his father wasn't available for practice, he would go to the gym and, by himself, invent special moves and shots. He knew just about every "book" move there was, and he felt the need to cook up something with the unique stamp of Pete Maravich on it.

Pete usually worked alone. Who could help him with the things he was trying to do? Anyway, as he said years later, "When you are in a gym by yourself, you can do anything you want. So I began fooling around with the ball, doing funny things. I would get tired just shooting straight to the basket or dribbling around in circles. So I practiced different stuff that was exciting to me and much more fun. I would throw the ball off the wall and try to make a basket. I would bounce it off the floor and up to the rim. I would even throw it over the rafters and try to bank it in."

And when *that* kind of playing around became boring, Pete began creating even wilder antics. One would begin with Pete whipping the ball behind his back, then between his legs and around his neck, and end with a snap pass aimed at a certain spot on the wall. In addition, he tried — and usually sank — all kinds of difficult shots, and perfected flashy passes and startling dribble-stop-and-shoot variations.

Finally he reached the point where he felt sure

he could do each of his tricks with steady success. So he told some boys about the crazy, funny things he had mastered. Naturally they wanted to see him perform, and he wanted an audience.

"Then, of course," he said, "when they'd come to see me do the stuff, I'd never make it. The ball would just not go in. I wasn't choking or anything, but I did get awfully uptight when the other guys would watch me try."

Whether he succeeded or failed, young Pete was always practicing: trying — and doing — glittering gems of basketball play that many adult players find difficult or impossible to do. While other boys his age were making model airplanes, working on stamp or coin collections, Pete was devoting every free minute to an activity that was much more than just a hobby to him. He wasn't yet in his teens, but basketball was the only future he could imagine for himself. Without a doubt, Pete was his father's dream come true.

Devoting all that time and effort to what he loved was a joy to Pete. But he was a perfectionist. When he wasn't able to work all the wonders he wanted to with a basketball, he was deeply upset. Pete himself has described one of those panicky upsets:

"I was 12 at the time, and one night I jumped out of the window with the basketball under my arm. I ran for three miles into the woods, and spent the night sleeping with the ball cradled in my arms."

Although he no longer remembers what brought on such a terrifying moment, Pete admits that he definitely was afraid.

And he had not yet played in his first school varsity game.

Basketball's Wonder Child

"STARTING AT ONE GUARD POSITION, wearing number five, Pete Maravich."

As the announcer's voice echoed through the gymnasium, a slender 14-year-old stepped onto the basketball floor. His hair was cut very short, in a crewcut, and his somewhat large ears looked even larger.

Students in the stands might have laughed, but there was determination in the set of Pete's jaw and fiery determination in the chocolate-brown eyes that seemed to say, "I'm a good player, so don't judge me by size and appearance."

If he was nervous, nobody else was aware of

it. But young Peter Press Maravich might well be nervous. This was his first game as a member of the varsity team at Daniel High School in Clemson. He was only a freshman, but he had cracked the starting lineup. The other four starters were two juniors and two seniors.

The official walked out to center court, the basketball under his arm. Daniel High and its opponents got set for the center jump; the ball went up — and the action began!

The two centers leaped into the air; the ball was tapped toward Pete, and he grabbed it. He dribbled toward the enemy basket, stopped, and flipped a pass to a teammate, then moved toward the basket. One of Daniel High's forwards took the shot and missed. The other team got the rebound and raced up court.

The agile figure of five-foot-three, 85-pound Pete Maravich bounded up and down the court. One of the smallest boys in the game, he still tried to wedge his way close to the basket for rebounds. And never did he back off when a bigger and stronger opponent drove toward him, hoping to scare the "little guy" away. Pete did his best, but his team lost by one point.

The loss hurt Pete's pride, but something else about his first varsity game hurt him even more. Not once did the other four players on his team pass the ball to him. Didn't they like him? Did they think he wasn't good enough? Or were they afraid that he — a freshman — might show them up?

Whatever the reason, it was a sad young man who entered the Maravich home that night. There were tears in his eyes as he told his father what had happened. But he hadn't lost his confidence. He said defiantly, "If they had passed the ball to me, we would have won. I can shoot."

In his second game a short while later, Pete got a chance to show what he could do. He played guard, and this time the ball was passed to him. He made the most of his opportunities by passing well and shooting accurately.

It was a tough, well-played contest. The high point of the game came in the final seconds of the see-saw battle. With the score tied and the seconds ticking away, Daniel High's center plucked a rebound off the backboard and snapped a pass to Maravich. Pete was off and dribbling. He sneaked his way past one defender, cut past the midcourt line, veered to the right side of the floor, glanced at the basket, and stopped. He bounced the ball off the floor, leaped clear of a defender, and arched a one-hander at the hoop — from 20 feet away. The ball struck the front of the rim, hopped against the backboard, and dropped through the net — two points and a spectacular, last-second victory for Daniel High.

The successful 20-foot tie-breaker not only won the game. It also won for Pete the respect and admiration of those who had doubted the "skinny kid" could do the job. His teammates decided they had been foolish to keep the ball away from him in the first game. But the win meant more to Pete than to anyone else. It wasn't enough for just Pete to know he could shoot; it was terribly important that everyone else know it too. And now they did.

Life as the son of a basketball coach was good for Pete, determined as he was to play top-notch basketball. The bad side was that coaches often change jobs; they have to move from one town to another, and their sons have to shift from one school to another. This could be hard on a boy like Pete, who didn't find it easy to make new friends.

By 1962 the 14-year-old had become buddies with several boys in Clemson. But now he would have to start over again in Raleigh, North Carolina, where Press Maravich took the assistant coaching job at North Carolina State.

However, it was a move up the coaching ladder for his father, and that delighted Pete.

Soon the talented teen-ager discovered it wasn't so hard for him to make friends after all. His ready smile and basketball skills combined to make him popular. As he made friends at Raleigh's Needham-Broughton High School, Needham-Broughton found it had a basketball prodigy on its varsity.

Pete was still so thin he appeared to be suffering from malnutrition. His weight could not keep up with his rapid growth, and any shots Pete took more than 15 feet from the basket required a special effort and all the muscle he could muster. At times he actually started his shot close to the floor — but the ball regularly swished through the hoop more often than it missed. Just how often is reflected in his senior-year scoring average: 32 points a game!

Needham-Broughton had a winner in Pete Maravich, although N-B basketball coach Olin Broadway may have wished Pete was a bit more coachable. Pete had a mind of his own, and his remarkable talent usually persuaded his coaches to see things his way.

"In high school," Pete said, "I had four different coaches in four years, and they never gave me much argument about my stuff. . . . I always put it to them this way: If I can get the ball to a man with a pass behind my back as well as I can with a regular chest pass, what's the difference?"

From the start of his basketball career, Pete's playing was regarded with mixed feelings by both coaches and teammates. It was true that he could perform magic with a ball, whether he was passing, dribbling, or shooting. On the other hand, his independent ways antagonized people. Basketball is a team sport, Coach Broadway and others would tell him. It's great for you to play as well as you do, but what about the rest of the team? What good does it do us if you score 30 points and we lose? And how do you think it makes the other players feel when you try to be a one-man team?

The arguments made sense to everyone but Pete. His attitude then, and for several years afterward, was: "Sure, I come out to win the game. That's always number one. But I also want to put on a performance the fans will enjoy."

Pete was a much better player than the other boys he played with, and he knew it. So the choices to him seemed to be: (1) Play your best. That's the only way to play, so don't worry about what anyone will say. Or (2) don't use all your skills. Be the "good guy" and give the others a chance to shine too.

Pete made the first choice — play your best.

And his best meant challenging an entire rival team with cometlike dribbling the length of the floor and finishing with a driving layup that would leave defenders standing flat-footed in his wake. His best crowd-rousing, totally unpredictable passes not only staggered opposing players but also took his own teammates by surprise. So did his whirlwind bursts to the basket — a variety of one-handed hook shots and outside jumpers, with uncanny marksmanship from all angles of the court against an assortment of blanketing defenses.

By his senior year at Needham-Broughton, the name Pete Maravich was almost as well known in the South as Robert E. Lee. Pete averaged 32 points a game in his last year. He had polished his ball-control to a professional level. He had repeatedly tested himself against the best opposition available — including one-on-one match-ups with college stars from nearby Clemson — and he always won.

As a basketball player, Pete Maravich was more than ready for college. But his family decided he should wait a year before selecting his college.

"I think," a friend said, "his parents felt that a year at prep school would help Pete mature. All that basketball success had made him pretty sure of himself. But he wasn't so grown-up when he didn't have a basketball in his hands."

And so, after being graduated from Needham-Broughton, Pete continued to practice anywhere he could find a hoop. He could hardly wait for the basketball season to begin at Edwards Military Academy — the prep school in Salemburg, North Carolina, his family had selected for him.

It took Pete only one game with his new team to show them he was a basketball genius. Within a few games, he had prepared everyone at school for a record-shattering performance.

In one contest between Edwards Military and a rival prep school, Pete did everything but referee the game. On play after play, he charged across the mid-court line, amusing the fans with his behind-the-back moves or his between-the-legs dribble. Razor-sharp passes darted from his hands to teammates cutting for the basket. Points rolled off his fingertips on jump shots from in close and far out, on explosive drives to the hoop, on acrobatic twisters that flew at the net from everywhere on the floor. And whenever the rival coach tried to smother him with two or three players, Pete responded with cunning fakes that left them helpless.

When the massacre was over, Edwards Military had acquired another scalp, and Pete had recorded 50 points plus a lot of assists and rebounds. It isn't often that any player scores that many points in a game, and it seemed an almost unreal score for a prep-schooler.

Memorable as that 50-point splurge was, the high point of Pete's single season at Edwards Military came in a nonprep league contest against the freshman team at North Carolina State.

There was a special attraction to the game for Pete: his father was varsity coach at NCS. And, even though Press had little officially to do with the NCS freshman squad, the game was regarded as a personal match between Pete and his father.

It came as a shock, especially to the college squad, when Pete spearheaded an attack that swamped NCS, 90-53. A prep team beat a lineup of older, more experienced players by 37 points! It was unexpected and almost unheard of!

The show put on by Pete in that game, described again and again by sports fans, piled still more fame on the kid with the floppy socks and flashy style of play. In fact, it came almost as an anticlimax that Pete was selected to the Prep All-America team. He was being written about now as "Pete the Pistol," with his boosters insisting that nowhere else in the country was there a faster, more accurate "gun" with a basketball.

Father and Son

ON THE BASKETBALL COURT, Pete had his own world, and in it he was king. He had press clippings that said it was so. Family and friends constantly assured him it was true. He was admired by many people who idolize sports stars. But some basketball fans didn't admire his way of playing the game. They said he was a "ball hog" who never gave the other players a chance.

More than one of these critics laid the blame directly on Press Maravich. Nothing, they felt, was more important to "Papa" Maravich than his son's career. They said that Press had pushed the boy into a basketball career almost from birth, and that he fed Pete's vanity. It was always, "Pete did this," and "Pete's going to do that."

The criticisms grew more intense as the time came for Pete to name his college — the one for which he would play basketball.

The young superstar had received offers from many colleges but so far hadn't shown a preference. Wasn't it Press, critics asked, who was turning down the offers because *he* wasn't invited to come with his son, as the varsity basketball coach for the same school?

Looking back at the game in which Edwards Military had trounced Press' North Carolina State freshmen, critics also wondered if father and son were becoming rivals. When Pete's team had won, sportswriters insisted that Pete's joy at the win showed there was trouble brewing between the Maraviches. They quoted Pete: "It was something — our taking State that way. I mean, after they gave the game the big father-against-son buildup. You just have to believe it made winning that much more enjoyable."

But Pete's reaction could simply mean that, as a normal teen-ager, he was trying to break away and be more independent. No matter how well he had played, there had always been someone to remind him that his father, Press the Pro, had coached him from the time he was a small child. Pete could very well be thinking, "It's time people started giving *me* credit for all those hours of practice."

Even Pete's harshest critics admitted that Pete was a one-in-a-million player with a great future. One said, "If this kid ever puts as much effort into playing defense as he puts into clowning and shooting, he could be the greatest guard who ever wore a pair of shoes." But, he added, "he's got to learn there are four other kids out there with him, wearing the same uniform. Will he?"

Pete himself was having too much fun and success to listen to suggestions for better team play and defensive tactics. Offensive play was Pete's key to getting ahead. So what if his opponents picked up a few baskets because of his defensive lapses? Didn't he often score more by himself than the entire other team?

While Pete was still weighing a stack of offers from colleges throughout the country, his father was invited to coach Baltimore's pro team — the Bullets in the National Basketball Association. Baltimore wanted Press because he was a fine coach. But also they counted on Coach Maravich persuading Pete to join him when Pete was through college. Pistol's dynamic play would not only improve the team; it would also bring in a lot more fans.

But Press made it known that he wanted to go to the college Pete decided on. For a short time Pete considered West Virginia. That was the school where Jerry West had built his reputation before going on to many seasons with the NBA's Lakers. Would the father-and-son team split up after all?

Then the Maraviches ended the guessing game by announcing they would both be going to Louisiana State University.

For Press the decision was really startling. Few college coaches would refuse a chance to coach a team like the Bullets. But Press chose to pass up the fame and salary of a professional coach to direct a college team. It looked as though he was putting Pete's future above his own.

As for Pete, he must have been tempted by the opportunity to be independent, to be his own man at a college apart from his father. But he knew how much that decision would have hurt his father's feelings. And he also recognized his own need for a dependable coach and adviser.

When Pete finally told a reporter he would be wearing the colors of Louisiana State, his statement was simple and direct: "I wanted to play for my father, and I think he always wanted to coach me. We knew how tough it would be on both of us if we went to the same school, but the chance to revive basketball at LSU seemed like an appealing challenge."

Press' words almost echoed those spoken by his son. "I always wanted to coach Pete," Press said, "and when I took the job at LSU I was anxious to have him with me. I knew he could give their basketball program a big boost in a hurry."

"The Fastest Gun
in the South"

"MARAVICH IS LIKE COUSY. What's more, even
though he's so young, he may even be better
than Cousy."

That surprising opinion was expressed by a
magazine writer who had seen Bob Cousy star
for many championship years with the Boston
Celtics. Cousy's dynamic style was well known
to the other men present, but they had never
seen the LSU freshman play. Two of them had
never even heard of Maravich.

They asked the writer to explain how he could
possibly compare a teen-ager who had just

finished high school with one of the finest all-around guards in NBA history?

"OK," said the writer. "Cousy controlled the ball so well, he could beat most pro guards in a man-to-man situation. Most, but not all of them. This kid Maravich is unstoppable. He can make a basketball do things you wouldn't believe. He doesn't just control the ball, he *owns* it."

The men moved closer as the writer continued, "I saw him in a game last year, and you had to see it to believe what happened. Both guards and one forward on the other team tried all game to lock him up. They did everything except hold the kid's hands at his sides. Nothing worked. He dribbled with either hand, changed speeds and direction like a motor scooter. I felt as if I were watching a man playing against a bunch of grade-schoolers."

The writer paused and raised his right hand, as if taking an oath. "Right now," he said, "Maravich could go against Cousy at his best and wear him out."

If Pete had been present at the conversation, he probably would have agreed. He felt he was now more than ready to meet the best guard in the world in a man-to-man match-up.

One day Pete and a friend watched a pro game on television. One of the teams was the

Philadelphia 76ers, who had the high-scoring and excellent defensive guard, Hal Greer. A few seconds after the end of the game — in which Greer scored 23 points and held his man to 12 — Pete snatched up his basketball and rushed out to the back-yard court.

Flipping in one-handers, cutting and spinning around the backboard while the ball did blurringly fast and magical things, young Maravich challenged Greer and other phantom players — the best he could imagine. Jerry West . . . Oscar Robertson . . . Cousy . . . And, as the ball whispered through the net on shot after fantastic shot, it was obvious he was winning every battle.

When Pete, exhausted but triumphant, finally took a break and came to the sideline, he was still dribbling the ball. His eyes were glowing with the flame of competition, and his slender frame was a coiled spring still quivering to go-go-go.

"Neat moves, Pete," said the friend who had watched the game with him. "Keep it up and you'll be like Greer in a couple more years."

Pete's eyes widened with a far-away look. "I'd like to go one-on-one against him right now."

"It was at that moment," the friend said later, "that I knew it would break Pete's heart if he didn't make the pros. As far as he was concerned, he wasn't dreaming and he wasn't bragging. In his head, he didn't need any more time to be ready for anyone."

What showed in Pete was pure faith in himself. It's the kind of faith that makes a player a champion — if he has the talent to go with it. And Pete did. "I'm not cocky," said Pete, when asked about his self-confident manner. "A cocky player is one who thinks he's good . . . but isn't."

Pete was proud of his real accomplishments and he felt he had earned the right to be proud. "My father taught me everything when I was a kid, it's true. And so all I had to do was practice." But, Pete added, while he valued what his father had done for him, he also felt he deserved credit for all his years of work and practice. "That was the hard part," Pete insisted. "Practice. Every day, every week, every month. Practice. When I was real young, I started working on ways to make a behind-the-back pass. I didn't look to the easy ways in trying to learn how. Like, I didn't turn to the side and throw the ball behind my back. That's no good. Anybody, even a four-year-old can pick up a toy and throw it behind his back like that.

"When I felt I had it right, practicing alone, I used it in practice with others. Then I'd try to throw it by the defender, facing him the whole time, so it would be a lot easier to pass in tight situations."

Whether he was playing by himself or with competition, Pete would work on his behind-the-back passes at least 15 minutes a day. Then he would practice throwing it as he took one step back, another move in a "real-game situation."

"The main thing to remember on this pass," he said, "as on any other pass, is to get it to the man you're throwing it to. If you really want to be good at it and to be able to count on it as a weapon in a game, you have to work on the behind-the-back pass every day. And you have to do it using both the right hand and the left hand. Then, when you've got it going good, try developing your behind-the-back bounce pass."

Even as a high-schooler, Pete didn't "fool around" with a basketball unless it helped to improve his game. The crazy things he did when dribbling or passing in a game were far from crazy because they so often led to baskets. The odd-looking moves he made in workouts, he explained, "are more than just for show. They stimulate my quickness and reaction."

There was one crowd-pleaser he performed while ball-handling on the run. Without interrupting his dribble, he would flick his wrist and zip the ball through a tangle of players. It would seem reckless, but the ball would fly straight and true, right into the hands of a teammate moving into perfect position for a shot.

Another skill he sharpened to a fine edge was designed to defeat a tight press put on him by two or three players at the same time. When this mismatch occurred, Pete would dribble the ball from hand to hand, shift direction slightly, then swiftly swing the ball behind his back. As it slid from one hand to the other, Pete's defenders would need a fraction of a second to adjust their thinking. That brief pause was all Pete wanted. *He* knew what was coming next, they didn't. And in the half tick of the clock that it took for his rivals to react, he was by them, angling his whippetlike body toward the basket.

"The move that really had the fans screaming was his hesitation step," said a teammate of Pete at Edwards Military Academy. "We'd watch him practicing it, going from a high dribble to a low one, then back again to the high one. After a while he got so good, he looked like a yo-yo champion going through his routine — only with a basketball.

"Then, not long after, there he'd be, using it in a game. He'd bring the ball upcourt and wait for one of their guards to hurry out to meet him.

Sometimes it would be both guards. Anyway, Pete would keep on coming, sort of slow, bouncing the ball about hip high, setting the guy up for this move. Then he'd take a sort of hesitating step, like he'd stumbled, at the same time changing the bounce of the ball about four or five inches higher. The other guy had to hesitate too. His rhythm was changed, and he couldn't make up his mind what to do. That's when Pete could fly for the basket, really faking the guy out of his shoes, leaving him standing there with his mouth open while Pete went zooming by."

The hesitation play worked often enough to upset the balance of the steadiest opponent. It gained Pete the extra step that usually spelled the difference between success and near-success. And when he combined the hesitation with the change-of-height in his dribble, he was doing twice as much to upset a defender's timing.

All of Pete's surprises of ball-control and body-control created a strong bag of tricks. But they wouldn't have meant very much if Pete hadn't usually succeeded in putting the ball in the basket. Because he could do it all, he earned the reputation of being a near-complete player as a 17-year-old.

Yet even as a teen-ager who loved to play the clown on the court, there was a level-headed approach to everything Pete did. As he said, recalling the workouts he held with himself, "I figured that the people in the pros and in college must have worked hard. Otherwise they wouldn't have earned a scholarship and they wouldn't have been able to make a living at this game."

Working hard also meant developing a proper attitude for playing the game. Part of a proper attitude was "staying loose." To illustrate one of the ways in which he loosened up, Pete would start to spin the ball on his fingertips. To most observers it would appear that this kind of trick had nothing to do with on-court action . . . until Pete described its value. "It helps me to relax my mind and body. If a player isn't loose, he just can't get himself and the ball to do the things he wants them to."

As he talked, Pete would spin the ball on his index finger, then keep the spin alive while transferring the ball from finger to finger. He could keep it twirling for as long as he wanted to — five minutes . . . 10 . . . 15 . . . And by the time he was ready to put it down, there wasn't a tense muscle in his body. Of course, while he was getting looser, his audience was getting tenser, waiting for the ball to spin out of control or for Pete's finger to develop a cramp.

Pete took a special delight in demonstrating

his wide-angle vision. The kind of eyesight (which enabled Bob Cousy to make *his* startling "blind" passes) allowed Pete to look straight ahead while dribbling, yet, at the same time, to see everything that was taking place on both sides *and* a good portion of the court behind him. He often took fans — and teammates — by surprise with a cross-court pass thrown far to his left or right while his eyes seemed to be focusing dead ahead. But the really breath-stopping part of his act came when he would be driving toward two or three defenders near the basket. As he came within five feet of them and they moved to engulf him, Pete would flip the ball back over his shoulder to a teammate. This lay-off pass would be so unexpected that the player with the ball was usually free to go the rest of the way for an uncontested layup.

To understand wide-angle vision, try this test. Stand and raise your hands until they are about six inches from your ears. You should be able to see them by looking out the corners of your eyes. Now start to slowly move the hands back. If you have normal vision, the hands will disappear from view after you have moved them back about four inches. Players like Pete Maravich, and there are very few with his kind of vision, are able to see their hands far beyond the four-inches-back point.

Pete enjoys talking about basketball and about the things he does with a ball. But he will always make the point that no basketball player is ready to try complex drills until he has learned the basic movements of the sport. He will say, for example, that there are three basic elements in passing — fingertip control, backspin, and follow-through. And before anyone can learn any of the fancy, difficult techniques, he has to develop the four fundamental passes everyone uses: the chest pass, the bounce pass, the overhead pass, and the baseball pass.

Pete had learned his lessons well. Now he was about to put his skills to a new test as a member of LSU's Tigers.

The All-Star Freshman

WHEN THE MARAVICH father-and-son team arrived at Baton Rouge, they weren't met by a mob of adoring fans. In fact they weren't recognized; they might have been tourists for all the reporters seemed to care.

For Press Maravich, Pete's father, this indifference was shocking. Although Pete would not be eligible for the varsity until his sophomore year, the new basketball coach of the Tigers wanted everyone to recognize his son immediately. The boy was going to bring nationwide fame to the university. Not since the days of Bob Pettit, who had gone on to become one of professional basketball's greatest forwards, had LSU featured a star of such brilliance.

So Press immediately started a one-man Pete Maravich campaign. Whenever he could, he would sing his sons's praises to newsmen. The school's going to build a new arena for Pete, he told them, and he's going to bring in so many fans that you'll forget they play football here. (The LSU football team was nationally famous.) "Just wait until you see my boy," Press repeated again and again. But for all his efforts Pete's father got, from fans and newsmen alike, the same reaction as from one writer who said: "Let's wait and see. We've seen a lot of hotshot high school phenoms fade when they move up to playing against tougher competition."

Pete continued to practice, waiting for the basketball season to begin. He felt disappointed because he and his father had thought the team would practice and play all home games in the Coliseum, LSU's modern arena. Instead, they learned, the Tigers would be using the University High School gym for almost a month-and-a-half at the beginning of the season.

Pete asked his father if there was any way they could convince university authorities to let them practice on the LSU court.

"No chance," Press told him. "They're using the Coliseum for a horse show for those weeks. And at the end of the season, there's a rodeo scheduled to be in there. That means we have to arrange our last games to be played out-of-town."

But the Maraviches were at LSU, and together they'd change everything. Press, with his fine coaching of the varsity team, would shape the Tigers into a threat in the Southeast Conference. And Pete, right from his freshmen year, would put the names of LSU and Maravich on sports pages across the country.

Although it took the national newspapers a while to catch up with what was happening at LSU, the local sports pages were very soon reporting on the Pete Maravich Show.

In the words of one Baton Rouge reporter: "By the time the freshman season started, you could hardly get a ticket for the games. Just as soon as Pete began to put on his exhibitions during his first week of workouts, the freshmen were practicing to standing room only. Right away, everybody on campus was saying that boy from Carolina really was something else. They came to see his shooting, and he gave 'em every shot you could think of — and a few you couldn't. But what really floored one and all was the crazy things he did with the ball. Why, his passing alone was worth the price of admission!"

Of course, Pete had his critics, here too. One local fan remembered the way Bob Pettit had taken his one-handed jump shot. He compared it to the way Pete took his. "Pettit," the critic reminded Pete, "was one of the best, and he always held the ball from underneath just before he let go of the ball. The way you do it looks like something players were doing back in the 1940's."

It did resemble the style of the "old-time" players who always had thrown the ball at the basket with two hands. But young Maravich had a sensible explanation. "I've always shot that way," he replied, "because the most important thing is to be a two-eyed shooter. By putting my left hand to the side, instead of underneath, I take it out of my line of vision. That means I've got both eyes focusing on the basket. You've got to have two eyes looking at something to have depth perception."

As for the passing, some people called it "hot-dogging." But even if it looked like showing off, Pete seldom failed to whip the ball where he wanted it to go.

The freshman team's coach, Greg Bernbock, was never heard to complain about Pete's style. And the varsity coach, proud Press Maravich, would just grin whenever someone mentioned Pete's passing wizardry. "That kid of mine," he would say, "he won't hit the open man unless the man's under the basket for a layup. Pete's always looking to pull off these passes the hard way instead of the easy way. But he always comes through, doesn't he?"

There wasn't anyone to argue that; Pete came through in game after game as the Tiger freshmen put together a season of 16 wins and one loss. And that losing effort, a 75-74 squeaker, came in the last contest against a strong squad from Tennessee, played on Tennessee's home court.

That game was one time Pete did fail to come through. It had gone down to the last eight seconds, with LSU trailing 75-73, when Pete was fouled. It was a one-and-one foul situation, which meant he would be entitled to a second foul shot only if he made the first.

The pressure felt by his teammates was clear on their faces as they lined up on both sides of the foul lane. As Pete stepped to the foul line, he alone seemed relaxed and confident. The pro-Tennessee fans started a chorus of sound intended to upset Pete. He merely smiled, bounced the ball a couple of times, and flipped it through the hoop. 75-74.

The referee caught the ball on the second

bounce and handed it to Pete for the bonus shot. His teammates got set for an attempt at the rebound in case he missed, although the expression on his face said, "Calm down, I won't miss."

The crowd noises started again. Pete bounced the ball again, brought it into position for the shot, narrowed his eyes at that basket, and flipped the ball at the hoop. The basketball arced up, slightly to the left. It hit the inside of the metal ring, slid around to the right side, seemed about to spin in — and dropped out. A cheer rocked the stands as a Tennessee player snatched the ball out of the air. LSU tried in vain to regain control as the clock ticked away its chance at a perfect season.

Pete pushed his way through the crowd and disappeared into the locker room. By the time his father got there to congratulate him on scoring 31 points and to help him get over the dissappointment of losing, his son had vanished. Press searched for a while, then returned to the hotel where the team was staying in Knoxville. There, in his room, he found Pete. Where had Pete gone after the game? "I left the field house by myself," he explained in a voice thick with emotion. "I walked the two miles back here."

"I should have figured it," was Press' reaction. "When I was playing for Aliquippa High and

Rochester beat us, I walked 12 miles back to town."

Although the 1966-67 season had ended on a sour note for Pete, he had sung a merry tune in all the games before the last. He had hit for a season-high total of 66 points against the Baton Rouge Hawks. He had poured in 741 points in 17 games, for a per-game average of 43.6. He had averaged almost 10½ rebounds and close to seven assists a game. Add to that his 45 percent shooting average and it was clear that the LSU varsity — and its coach — had a lot to look forward to in 1967-68.

Pete Rewrites
the Record Books

THE SHOWING OF Louisiana State's varsity basketball team for the 1966-67 season had been miserable. While Pete had been doing wonders for the freshman squad, his father had suffered as his varsity five staggered through the season of three wins and 23 losses. It was with high hopes that Press welcomed his son's arrival on the team at the beginning of the 1967-68 court year.

For the first game of the season the student body swarmed in to see the sophomore star in action. His fans were filled with school spirit, and Pete promised to make LSU a winner.

The team's first opponent on the schedule was

Tampa. According to a Baton Rouge newspaper evaluation: "LSU was starting the season with an easy one. It looks like the Maravich-led Tigers will breeze all the way, putting notch number one on the Pistol's gun."

Standing on the court just before the opening tap, the Pistol was relaxed. He had just finished amusing the crowd with his customary warm-up show. Fancy dribbling. The ball-twirling exercise. Successful shots from different spots on the floor. Now the six-foot, five-inch, 180-pound young star, wearing the number 23, stood smiling at his father. Press Maravich smiled back. But it was rather a tight smile; he felt less relaxed than his son.

Then the game was under way, and it didn't take Pete long to put his team in charge. His large brown eyes glowing under his flying brown hair, he scorched the net with jump shots, layups, and one-pointers from the foul line. He grinned happily as his passes connected with teammates to complete plays for baskets.

By the end of the contest, Press Maravich's smile was broad and contented. Pete and his teammates had downed Tampa, 97-81. To make things perfect, Pete had shown none of the usual jitters of a sophomore starting his first varsity game. The Pistol had connected for 20 field goals and eight of nine shots from the foul line, for a total of 48 points. He also had snared 16 rebounds, a fine total for a center but a whopping one for a guard. In addition, Pete had four assists.

The next day's sports pages were off and raving about "LSU's sharp-clawed tiger." The 48-point total, particularly, was the main subject of the game accounts. One writer said, "It's just a matter of time — and not much of that — before Maravich breaks Bob Pettit's single-game scoring mark." Pettit's Southeast Conference high, 58 points in a game played in the early 1950s, had been considered untouchable. But as the writer went on to point out: "As a freshman, Pete racked up totals of 66, 57, 53, and, three times, 50. Which means it's not a question of *if* he'll break Pettit's mark, but *when*."

Meanwhile Pistol Pete continued to shoot the eyes out of the basket. The next game saw him pour in 42; then 51 in the third match of the season. After that came totals of 42, 42, 46, 58, 30, 55, 32, 42, 52, 33, 52, 54, 44, 21, and 49.

But there were people who dismissed his sensational point-making. They pointed out that LSU wasn't showing such a sensational record as a team. Of those first 18 games, in which Pete had averaged slightly better than 44 points a game, LSU had lost eight times.

Some of the criticism was directed against Pete's lack of defensive play. "He does a lot when he has the ball," was one comment, "but nothing much when the other team has it."

Pete's response to these remarks was, "I don't think I play bad defense. I'm a gambler." And a gambler in basketball, according to Pete's logic, wins some of the time and loses some of the time.

Press, to no one's surprise, defended his team — and especially his son. He found it hard to understand how anyone could complain after comparing this season's team with the previous season's when the Tigers managed to win only three games. This year, after only 18 games of a 26-game schedule, his boys already had won 10. Moreover, LSU had beaten such tough opponents as Alabama, Auburn, Tulane, Clemson, and Mississippi State. What, he wondered, do you have to do to satisfy the critics?

The answer was supplied by a national magazine article, which scolded Press Maravich for failing to control his son's total self-dedication. "While the hotshot Pistol is shooting away, his teammates are wasting away with nothing to do but watch his antics and double-figure scoring."

What the Pistol was aiming at, a newspaperman insisted, was the all-time NCAA scoring record set by Frank Selvy of Furman University.

Selvy had averaged 41.7 points a game over a full season for the record. At the rate Pete was going, he stood an excellent chance of surpassing Selvy.

Neither Pete nor his father denied they would like to see Pete top Selvy. And instead of trying to avoid more criticism by shooting less, Pete shot as much as ever and continued to stage the nationally famous Pete Maravich Show.

"That's really what basketball is for me," Pete declared, "an entertainment, a chance to express myself. It's what I've chosen to do in my life. It's my thing.

"The people at LSU and Baton Rouge, and all over the Southeastern Conference — they know me. And they know that when Pete Maravich comes out on the court, it's show time. Sure I come out to win the game. That's always number one. But I also want to put on a performance the fans will enjoy. I never go into a game thinking, 'Oh, here's another 40 minutes to kill. I'll just go out, run around, and then head back to the shower.' "

Pete was satisfied with the way he was playing the game. He was also satisfied with the way the season was going for him personally. Most of the fans weren't complaining. And his father, whose job was to produce a winning team, wasn't telling him to do anything different. So the sophomore star continued to play basketball in his wild, fancy, and always exciting way.

He shot when there were two enemy defenders playing him close, sometimes when there were three. He went for the basket from close range, from 20 to 25 feet away, even from distances of 35 and 40 feet. He varied his shots — sometimes jumpers, sometimes hooks, sometimes push shots, sometimes layups, sometimes weird twisters that had no name.

His scoring figures mounted steadily. By the time LSU had completed the first 20 games of the 1967-68 season, the Tigers had won 11 and lost nine. But the Pistol continued to fire away at Selvy's record. Against Florida and Georgia he scored 47 and 51 points respectively. That boosted his record-shattering pace to a 44.5 points-per-game average.

Game number 21 on the LSU schedule was against Alabama. The Alabama Field House was jammed from floor to ceiling. Not only did the fans want to see their home team beat Maravich & Company; they wanted to see Pistol Pete stopped cold.

Instead they saw the Pete Maravich who couldn't miss, ripping the net with 24 bull's eyes out of 52 attempts from the field. Added to those

48 points were 11 out of 13 successful free throws, for a total of 59 points.

After the game, won by LSU, 99-89, Pete stood waving at center court as the appreciative Alabama fans applauded him wildly. These were lovers of fine basketball. Even though 'Bama had lost, they had witnessed Southeastern Conference history. They had seen the Pistol gun his way past Bob Pettit's old mark to set a new SEC single-game scoring record.

Back in the dressing room, Pete slapped teammate Ralph Jukkola on the back. Jukkola grinned and said, "Glad to do it, Pete,"

What Jukkola had done was to make it possible for Pete to score the record-shattering basket in the last seconds of the game. Alabama had possession of the ball under the LSU basket and unless the Tigers could get it quickly, and Pete could shoot, there would be no new record. That was when Jukkola had stolen the ball from Alabama at midcourt.

"I was really surprised," said Maravich. "I grabbed the pass and heard Ralph screaming at me to shoot. I guess instinct took over then, because all I remember is stumbling toward the basket and letting loose a desperate two-hander."

The *swish* of the ball through the basket came next, followed by the booming roar from the packed field house.

That same night, as Pete was being congratulated in one corner of the dressing room, a reporter was talking to another LSU player in a different part of the room. One of the questions the reporter asked of Jeff Tribbett, who happened to be Pete's roommate, was, "Doesn't it bother the other boys that Pete gets all the credit? Wouldn't you like to grab some headlines too?"

Tribbett paused in the middle of tying a shoelace, thought for a moment, and shook his head. "No, it doesn't bother me. Pete earns everything he gets. If any of us was that good, we would get the headlines."

"You mean everyone on the team feels the same way you do?" the reporter asked. He obviously couldn't believe Pete was so popular with his teammates.

"We have a job to do on this team," Tribbett replied. "And if we didn't want Pete to score so much, we could make sure he didn't get the ball as much as he does. It's very simple. Pete has to shoot 40 times a game if we're going to win. He just has to. And we see that he does!"

Tribbett finished dressing, then told the reporter: "Our team stays together. We go to parties together. We date together. We watch TV together. We don't just like Pete — we admire him."

The admiration for Pete went beyond the limits of his team. It even went beyond the limits of LSU. Among the Pistol's most ardent boosters was the legendary Adolph Rupp, coach of the Kentucky Wildcats. After a midseason game in which Kentucky had defeated LSU, 109-96, Rupp said, "I just watched Maravich hit for 52 points against my boys. Now that's what I call shooting. I'd always said we wouldn't play him any way but one-on-one. But when I saw the way he was going at the beginning of this game, I told the boys to drop off the other LSU players and cover Maravich as much as they could. They tried, and you saw what happened. This boy is as near the complete basketball player as you'll see anywhere."

This was the kind of praise Pete loved. But as much as it must have pleased him to read Rupp's remarks, he didn't need any outside sources to inspire him. The fire that burned inside Pete Maravich was more than enough. Still shooting for Selvy's record, he maintained his torrid pace after the 59 points against Alabama with games of 34, 55, 40, 17 (against a defense-minded Tennessee team), and 42.

That completed the LSU schedule for the 1967-68 season. The team record stood at 14 wins and 12 losses. A marked improvement over the dismal

3-23 showing the previous year. But even more outstanding were Pete's personal achievements. He had scored 1,138 points in 26 games. That averaged out to 43.8 points a game, blasting Selvy's NCAA record by an average of 2.1 points a game!

Nationwide recognition of Pete's feat came swiftly. He was named to six All-America teams — by the Newspaper Enterprise Association, the Associated Press, United Press International, *The Sporting News*, *Look* magazine, and the National Association of Basketball Coaches.

United Press International also named him as runner-up in its voting for Player of the Year.

Locally he was the runaway winner as Most Valuable Player both at LSU and in the Southeastern Conference. In addition, Pete was declared the top sophomore in the SEC by a poll of coaches, and the number-one shooter in the SEC by a poll of players.

It was almost unanimously agreed that Pistol Pete belonged right up there with the best players in the nation. And he was only a sophomore!

Pete's Star Is Dimmed

THE HONORS HEAPED ON him were further evidence to Pete that his one-man style of play was right. In response to the few who called him "selfish, smug, and headline-hungry," he lashed back angrily:

"Those people who razz me for my style are behind the times. They're giving me the business because I'm doing something they can't do. Besides, what they don't recognize is that the things I do are good for the game."

And in defense of Pete's high-flying "show time" performance, Press pointed out how much it had done for LSU basketball. In 1966, he said, fewer than 50 season tickets had been bought by the fans. But when Pete moved up to the varsity in his sophomore year, the stock of LSU basketball zoomed. Bud Johnson, the university's sports information director, expressed the same opinion.

The critics found it even harder to build a case against the Maraviches when Pete won the Star of Stars Award, presented to the best player in the annual East-West All-Star Game.

After the presentation, Pete observed: "That award wasn't for my shooting. I scored only 16 points. But I had 11 or 12 assists! From the coaches' and writers' standpoint — and they were the ones who voted for me — those assists seemed to be the highlight of the game. I know that's what the fans liked best."

It was important to Pete to please the fans, coaches, and writers, but especially in a game involving other top-rated players. "Any time you win that award over guys that are All-America," Pete said proudly, "it has to be the best. And it was all on my passing."

Then the Pistol tried out for the 1968 Olympic basketball team. Here was the chance for Pete to realize the dream of every young athlete. Of all the basketball players in America, he was one of the few offered an opportunity to represent the U.S. in the great international sport competition. In Mexico, as an Olympian, he could meet and get to know the finest athletes from many nations. He would see the sunny land south of the border, and be treated as a member of the team whose country had never lost an Olympic basketball game.

Dreams . . . Standing on the winner's platform and having a gold medal placed on his chest while the *Star-Spangled Banner* is being played . . . Thousands of people cheering . . . The returning hero . . . His family so proud of him. . . .

The invitation for the tryout came a week after Pete's award-winning East-West All-Star Game. Certain that he would be among the 12 players who would make up the U.S. team in Mexico City, Pete met his first disappointment shortly after he reached Albuquerque, New Mexico. When he showed up for practice, he learned that coach Hank Iba had placed him on the second team.

The LSU superstar with the highest scoring average in the nation was insulted. But he was determined to work his way up to the first team before the trials ended. He dug into his bag of tricks and put them all on display. But his flair for the dramatic move and stunning pass clashed with Coach Iba's strict ideas of how basketball should be played. To make things worse, Pete's

Following another 40-point game, Pete Maravich of Louisiana State, is greeted by his proud father-coach, Press Maravich.

UPI

Maravich, the all-time college scoring champ, adds two more points on a driving lay-up in an L.S.U. victory over Tulane.

Maravich works on his quick drive before a game in which he needs 40 points to shatter Oscar Robertson's scoring record.

Sidelined by injuries in National Invitational Tournament in New York, Maravich yells encouragement to his team on floor.

Joining Atlanta Hawks in the NBA, Maravich is tied up by Milwaukee, but a second later gets free for his first pro point.

As a pro, Maravich must also play tough defense. Here, Pete
goes up against Mike Davis of Buffalo before Davis can shoot.

As Dave Bing of Detroit Pistons crowds him closely, Maravich must decide in a split second how he'll get rid of the ball.

A ball hawk for the Atlanta Hawks, Maravich, above, pounces on a loose ball somebody else has lost. Below, Pete nimbly slaps the ball away from Walt Frazier of the New York Knicks.

style didn't sit well with Coach Iba's assistant, John Bach. Yet Pete knew no other way to play. He raced up and down the court in his usual loose, razzle-dazzle style. To some observers he seemed to be defying Bach's clear preference for ball-control and hard-nosed defense.

One sportswriter described Pete in action: "The moment he had the ball in his hands, he became the Pistol. The last thing he could do was operate like a robot. He was at his Globetrotter best. His passes were hitting other players dead-center, only they were usually unexpected. It often led to confusion. Pete's shooting was sharp, but his defense was kind of unsteady. And, of course, his dribbling was true to the Maravich motto of 'do what the fans like best.' "

What the fans liked didn't really make any difference there. The coach didn't like it. And when the cuts were announced, Pistol Pete's name was on the list of players to be left behind. He had good company. Also failing to make the 1968 Olympic squad were high-scoring All-America college stars Rick Mount of Purdue and Calvin Murphy of Niagara.

But Pete's ego was jarred, and he didn't hide his damaged feelings. "It was a real disappointment," he said on his return to Baton Rouge. "It was a once-in-a-lifetime thing and I missed it.

My father told me not to try out. Anyway, it doesn't make any difference to me now."

Pete's failure to make the Olympic team, however, supplied ammunition for his critics. One commented: "The double-barreled Maravich shotgun fired a noisy blank. Maybe he and his father won't be so cocky now."

Pete reacted to all the mud-slinging with: "Some of the things that have been written about me . . . well, I just have to think the writers never saw me play. But truthfully speaking, none of it bothers me. If I took it seriously, I'd be in a mental hospital right now."

Press Maravich's response was a mixture of anger and puzzlement. "The letters I get," he said. "You wouldn't believe the letters. They say I'm exploiting my son, or that I'm sacrificing the good of the team for my son. It shouldn't bother me, but it does. It's tough on me, and it's especially tough on my wife. It creates strain within the family."

Pete finally admitted it got to him too, that it had even begun to affect his relationship with Press. "If we lose," Pete said, "my father and I will discuss the game. Sometimes we disagree and my mother gets caught in the middle."

A New Orleans reporter reminded his readers of something that had happened earlier in the season. During a time-out in one of LSU's closest games, Pete had questioned the tactics Coach Maravich was directing the team to use.

Press, his face red with fury, had snapped at Pete, "I'm the coach here, and don't you forget it!"

But father and son had traveled a long road together. The more famous Pete became, the more public attention was focused on him — and his strong tie to his father. Their behavior at games was watched closely, and their comments were always news.

Some observers felt that Press' easy attitude toward Pete wasn't doing his son any good, wasn't preparing him to play for the pro coaches. They also felt that Press was demoralizing the other LSU players by his coach-as-fan attitude:

"I'm telling you, the things this boy can do with a basketball, why you wouldn't believe your eyes. I never know what he's going to do. It's like watching a great work of art. Sometimes I forget I'm coaching and just sit back to watch what's going to happen next."

But when several of the anti-Maravich critics hammered at the fact that no other coach would allow Pistol Pete to shoot as much as Press allowed him to, Pete flared back: "That's stupid! We're playing to win, and if I score big, we do pretty well."

He showed how LSU's won-lost record had

improved since they had arrived. Each was there to win for the school, Pete insisted for what felt like the millionth time. And both agreed that Pete had to shoot a lot if the team was to succeed. "There's a big difference between shooting 40 times a game and getting 40 good shots," Pete said.

If Pete wasn't able to simply smile at the critics and do his job, it was also true that having to defend himself against all attacks was an unfair burden for a 19-year-old to carry. It was enough to do to play a strenuous basketball schedule and attend classes.

I'd Rather Shoot Than Switch

AS THE NEXT COLLEGE YEAR began, Pete was looking to the future. "I forced too many shots as a sophomore," he said. "My 42 percent field shooting percentage can be improved. I'll do it this year."

It was clear that the better Pete played, the better LSU's Tigers would be. But comments like those of sports columnist Bill Carter of the Alexandria (Louisiana) *Daily Town Talk* continued. In one column, Carter wrote, "There is a growing suspicion . . . that Press and Pete . . . are 'using' LSU and that the university will realize more bad publicity than fame from this era."

LSU sports information director Bud Johnson supported Press and Pete. "There is always that question hanging over Press: Could he have got our program off the ground without Pete? I think the answer is yes. On the other hand, there is no doubt Pete's fame has helped the school. Our basketball team is known all over the country."

People might have expected Pete's teammates to agree with the criticisms. One Louisiana sportswriter wrote: "Press is extremely unpopular with the players, mainly because he recognizes nobody but Pete — and his caddies."

Among those so-called "caddies" — players in the lineup just to support Pete in his starring role — was Jeff Tribbett. Tribbett had played high school basketball alongside All-American Rick Mount in Indiana, and he was a fine player in his own right.

Tribbett said, "Coach Maravich has helped every boy on this team. So has Pete," he continued. "I know that they say Pete shoots a lot, but he gets open a lot too. When you're open, that's what you're supposed to do, put the ball up. Pete forces a few shots, but so do all basketball players."

"Do you feel you're a caddie for Pete?" Jeff was asked.

"It's a real privilege to play with someone like

Pete," was Tribbett's answer. "Pete got LSU in the limelight. We play before packed crowds everywhere we go. We play interesting basketball. This is just my opinion, but I'd rather watch a team like the Tigers than a slowdown brand [of the game] like they play at Tennessee."

LSU regular guard Rich Hickman commented: "You naturally have mixed emotions about playing with a superstar. But my strongest emotion is that I'm lucky to be on the same team with him."

Sportswriters, teammates, and fans who followed the fortunes of the LSU Tigers added their voices to the growing tide of pro-Maravich opinion. Women too, from coeds to the middle-aged, spoke fondly of Pete. They responded to him as basketball fans, taking delight in his bullet-swift moves and total confidence in any game situation.

They also responded to him personally. Thin and childish-looking, he had those large, sad-looking eyes, and more than one woman remarked that she would adopt him if she could.

The younger girls were won over by his casual, happy-go-lucky mannerisms. They liked his finger-combed long brown hair and his special trademark — floppy gray socks that he washed after every game.

The wife of an LSU official said, "I just don't know how to explain it. There has been a new interest in basketball since he came. You can see it everywhere driving around town, kids playing basketball. You never saw that before *they* came."

Last-Second Heroics

PETE & COMPANY opened the Tigers' 1968-69 season with a bang. Opponent number one was Loyola University of New Orleans. The magnetism of Pistol Pete had filled Loyola's Field House with 6,500 fans, something that hadn't happened since 1955. The attraction then had been Bill Russell leading a fine University of San Francisco team.

Loyola's game plan was clear from the opening tap-off. LSU's Jeff Tribbett grabbed the ball and flipped it to Pete, who immediately moved into enemy territory. But no Loyola player challenged him. Instead, as Pete dribbled the ball a full 25 feet from the basket, the opposition five stayed close to the backboard.

This was not going to be a game of man-to-man defense against LSU. Loyola was using a zone defense — determined to stop Pete from penetrating for any of his whirling drives and layups. He would have to earn his points on long-range marksmanship. The Pistol's only other choice was to pass off to his teammates, who were allowed to move through the barricade of bodies set up to block out Pete.

Pete passed to a teammate, took the return pass, and started bouncing the ball again. He was no stranger to the zone defense. He had faced it many times before. His eyes searched for a path through the screen Loyola had set up. None appeared. He dribbled a bit closer, until he reached a spot 20 feet from the basket. Suddenly two Loyola players slid toward him.

As Pete backed up a step or two, one of the players taunted, "Come on, gunner. Let's see how you shoot from there!"

A quick glance at the LSU bench told Pete his father also was annoyed by the Loyola strategy. "OK," Pete thought. "I'll shoot."

His sneakers squeaking on the boards, his socks flopping around his ankles, Pete shifted into high gear. Seconds later he had worked to a better position. Now Pete faced the basket directly, but somewhere between 25 and 30 feet away. Another bounce of the ball, a step forward, and then he leaped into the air. The basketball flew off his fingertips, looped, and dropped — right through the net.

Press Maravich slapped his hands together, satisfaction lighting his face. The LSU fans in the stands let out a cheer. Pete, grinning boyishly, trotted back on defense.

Loyola continued to use the stop-Maravich tactics, hopeful he would start missing. But Pete's pride was on the line, and he responded the way he knew best. After the Pistol had pumped in three shots from beyond the 25-foot mark, it was plain that the keep-away strategy was not going to work. It wasn't going to cool the "Fastest Gun in the South."

Midway through the first half, Loyola's coach changed his defensive maneuvers. His guards started coming out to meet Pete, but this didn't work either. It opened things up for Pete's teammates. He started snapping sharp passes to LSU players cutting toward the basket. It also allowed the Pistol to perform his famous show.

With the Loyola defense spread wider, Pete became a tornado. Jump shots from around the keyhole plunked through the hoop. Two-pointers registered time and again at the end of twisting, lightning dashes to the basket. Now and then there was a free throw when a Loyola player fouled the Pistol.

Nothing Loyola tried was good enough to shackle the scoring-passing machine named Maravich. When the coach again ordered his team to force Pete to shoot from the outside, Pete popped in four more goals from at least 25 feet — or found a teammate with a brilliant pass.

By the end of LSU's opening game, the Tigers had blown Loyola off the court, 109-82. Pete's part in the romp amounted to 52 points, coming on 22 field goals in 34 tries, and eight of nine from the free-throw line. It was a promise of good days ahead for Pete and LSU.

The Tigers' next game was against Clemson, the college for which Press had been varsity basketball coach during Pete's high school days. Clemson, playing on its home court, was "up" for the game. The team was out to show Press that they could play winning ball under a different coach.

Clemson's inspired squad put up a real battle. It went right down to the final buzzer. But LSU took the squeaker, 86-85, with Pete scoring 38 points.

Game number three on the 1968-69 schedule

was even tougher. It turned into a double-overtime struggle with a fired-up Tulane team edging LSU, 101-99. This was the first opportunity of the season for Pete's critics to open fire on him, and several immediately blamed the loss on Pete's "ball-hogging" and "show-off stunts."

Forward Ralph Jukkola spoke up as one of Pete's "neglected" teammates. He reminded people that he had played with prep All-Stater Don May at the University of Dayton and then compared Pete with May. "Pete and Don are two different kinds of players. May has to depend on someone getting the ball to him. Pete can do everything — shoot, rebound, handle the ball and get off a shot under extreme pressure."

Jukkola made it clear that Pete was the last person to blame for the loss to Tulane. And several other Tigers seconded Jukkola's opinion. They stated that it was great, playing alongside the Pistol. One remarked, "We know that, for every two baskets he scores, he'll be setting one of us up for a shot. We also know when he's double- or triple-teamed some of us will have to be open and that he'll get the ball to us. Like on those 11 assists he got in the Loyola game."

With this attitude going for them, the Tigers had no trouble getting back on the winning attack. Pete & Company next took on a strong

Florida five led by high-scoring Neal Walk. True to the Tiger tradition of that season, it was a see-saw battle that went into overtime. But this time the Tigers wrote a happy ending to the story, winning 93-89. The defeat was Florida's first after five consecutive wins.

Walk, in particular, came away from the game impressed with the all-around play of Pistol Pete. What impressed him most was the way Pete kept shaking loose from Florida's tough defense, to reach the basket for 45 points.

The season rolled on with LSU posting a record of seven victories in eight games. Victories over Wyoming, Oklahoma City, and Duquesne came in Oklahoma City, host for the All-College Tournament that year. This was coach Hank Iba territory — Iba, who had turned thumbs down on Pete for the Olympic team. Knowing that Iba would hear all about LSU's victory undoubtedly inspired Pete to outdo himself. The Pistol fired his way through the tournament for a per-game average of 46 points and a shooting accuracy of close to 50 percent.

Pete was also extremely pleased by the win over Duquesne. "We were the Cinderella team of that tournament," Pete said sometime later, "but the Dukes were pulling away from us in the last five minutes. Nobody went home, but it looked like curtains. Anyway, we fought back, and I hit a couple to pull us tighter. We were down by one with about a minute left when I drove the lane. I thought it was open at the time, but here came one of those two big Nelson brothers out of nowhere. I mean, those guys are huge and they're tough. Anyway, here he came, so I gave him a pump in the air and thought I was home free for sure. But, oh no. All of a sudden the other Nelson came flying at me and had me perfectly stuffed . . .

"I thought I was a goner. Well, I didn't yell out, 'It's show time,' or anything, but all I could do was give a couple of more pumps, bring the ball in tight to my chest, then flip it as I was going down onto the floor. The ball hit the side of the board and banked in. I couldn't believe it. The noise of the crowd blew me out, and we won the game.

"That was just an example of going to the show when it was necessary. Believe me, I didn't pull a zippety flip to entertain the Nelsons."

Maybe not, but as Bob Dellinger wrote in the *Daily Oklahoman*, "The All-College truly has never seen one like him, and it may be a long time before it does again."

The All-College Tournament, however, was the moment of greatest triumph for the Tigers that season. Right after it, they went into a tail-spin. Not even Pete's record-pace scoring could straighten them out. The Tigers lost game number nine to Alabama by three points, rebounded to slip past Vanderbilt by two points, then lost consecutive games to Auburn, Kentucky, and Tennessee.

Naturally the critics blasted Pete for these losses. They dismissed the fact that Pete was scoring more even though he was taking fewer shots. Instead they repeated their now familiar refrain, accusing Press and his "little gunner" of not caring whether LSU won or lost, so long as the Pistol scored well.

There was, of course, another side to the argument. As seen by Press Maravich, referees at games away from Baton Rouge were picking on Pete. Whether he was speaking as father or coach didn't really matter, he said. The important thing was that the referees were prejudiced against Pete.

"The boy's got to learn to settle down," said one referee after working a game at LSU's arena. "He's a great talent, but sometimes he tends to be a crybaby. He thinks a player can't block one of his shots or knock the ball out of his hands without committing a foul. He'd better mature before he gets to the pros."

Another referee said, "Pete isn't forcing the shots he did as a sophomore. His passing is as great as it ever was. He simply has to curb his temper, and that's where his father comes in."

While the bitter words went back and forth, the season continued. LSU won some, lost some, and arrived at the last game of their schedule with 12 wins and 13 losses. The contest was a crucial one. First, a victory would give the Tigers a .500 won-lost percentage for the season. If not great, it would certainly be a fine record against the high-caliber teams they played. Second, Press could not be accused of having a losing season. And third, Pete not only hated the idea of being part of a losing team but also he needed the game to score 49 points in order to top the all-time college scoring mark he had set as a sophomore.

LSU's opponent was the Georgia team they had beaten earlier in the season in Baton Rouge. But this time the game was in Georgia's arena, where the home team had a better feel for the court and the baskets, and the fans' cheering would give them an extra boost.

It was a tight contest most of the way. Then, in the second half, the Georgia Bulldogs began to pull away from LSU's Tigers. Things looked dismal for LSU as they fell behind by 15 points, until Pistol Pete found the range. He slashed the Georgia defense apart, ripping the nets to lead the surging Tigers. In one sizzling burst, he scored 13 straight points. When regulation time ran out the game was tied, 72-72.

In the first overtime, Georgia again edged ahead, only to have Pete hit a bucket with six seconds left on the clock to knot the game at 78 apiece.

Another five-minute overtime. This time, Pete took the game into his hands. He dribbled and passed flawlessly. His shooting was deadly. With the clock spinning toward the final minute, the Tigers were on top, 88-80. Then Pete relaxed and went into his show, eating up those last seconds by dribbling rings around the desperate Bulldog players.

As he avoided the grasping enemy hands, he paused every now and then to glance at the clock. At last, with just a few seconds remaining and the victory assured, Pete flicked a shot at the basket from 30 feet away.

The ball didn't touch any part of the hoop on its way through. The final score was 90-80, LSU. But the Tiger win had to take second place to an even more important story. The Pistol had scored 58 points on the night — 10 more than he needed to top the all-time scoring mark of his sophomore season. And it brought this season's total to 1,148.

Pete had played in 26 games and had averaged 44.2 points a game. The Pistol was competing with himself and winning. As a freshman, his average had been 43.6 points a game; as a sophomore, 43.8. And now as a junior, it was 44.2.

The Tigers' schedule in Pete's junior year had been pretty tough, but it hadn't stopped the Pistol from achieving his scoring goals. It also resulted in his earning another bundle of honors. He made the 1968-69 All-America teams of the Associated Press, United Press International, *The Sporting News*, *Look* magazine, Newspaper Enterprise Association, and the National Association of Basketball Coaches.

As for the Southeastern Conference, Pistol Pete was selected to the All-SEC First Team by the Associated Press, United Press International, and the SEC Coaches Poll.

Pete's awards reflected more than his ability to score at a hot pace. They honored him for the clutch player he proved to be throughout the season. For scoring the winning baskets in the last seconds of tight contests. For controlling the ball by dribbling wizardry in the final moments of close games.

The All-Time Scoring Champion

AMERICA'S BASKETBALL BUFFS were ready and waiting for the curtain to go up on the Pete Maravich Show as the 1969-70 collegiate season began. For three years Pete had given them great performances and great scoring. Now his fans wanted more — and better — from the college senior.

Weeks before LSU's opening game against Oregon State, Pete was like a hunting dog straining at his leash. This was his last year of college ball, and he knew the pro scouts would be watching closely. The more points he scored, the sharper his passes, the more he would impress them. That meant more money when the time came to talk contract with the NBA or ABA.

When Pete was asked if the most important thing on his mind was to show the scouts how valuable he was, he said he was concentrating on the season ahead. "Right now," he told a reporter, "I'm looking forward to two things this year. The first is trying again to get into a postseason tournament."

The National Collegiate Athletic Association tourney was just about out. Kentucky was also in the Southeastern Conference, and year after year Adolph Rupp's Wildcats were number one in the SEC. So it was almost certain that Kentucky would represent the SEC in postseason NCAA competition. But LSU still had a chance to reach the National Invitation Tournament (NIT) in Madison Square Garden, New York. If, as Pete observed, "we win enough games to rate a bid from the NIT."

Along with a postseason invitation, Pete's other aim for 1969-70 was "to break Oscar Robertson's three-year scoring record of 2,973. I've got 2,286," he said, "and if I stay healthy, maybe I can go after Oscar late in the season."

Asked if he would be changing his way of play, in case the pro scouts might want to see pure basketball instead of showmanship, Pete said nothing would be different. "Whatever happens," he said, "whatever the criticism, I'm going out shooting and passing in my own way. I can't change now. It's the only style I have, even if it's one long show. After all, everybody loves a show."

The show, and the season, got off to a fine start. LSU won its first four games, toppling Oregon State, Loyola, Vanderbilt, and Tulane. And in those tests, Pete hit for 43, 45, 61, and 46 points.

The Pistol's hand stayed hot as he netted 50 points in the next game, against Southern California. But it wasn't quite enough to offset a well-balanced USC attack, and LSU lost by a slim three-point margin, 101-98.

Then the Tigers came roaring back, with Pete collecting 49 and 46 points in the next two wins over Clemson and Oregon State. After seven contests, LSU boasted a 6-1 record and Pete was scoring at a per-game clip of 48.5 points a game!

Next on the schedule, however, was UCLA, the nation's top-ranked team. This was a team that fielded four players bound for the pros when their college careers were over. There was Steve Patterson, replacement at center for Lew Alcindor (Kareem Abdul-Jabbar); Curtis Rowe and Sidney Wicks at the forward positions; and John Vallely and Henry Bibby at the guard spots. And, as a John Wooden-coached team, it was a thoroughly drilled machine that played defense as well as it scored.

That was the team the Pistol tried to out-maneuver. Each time LSU had the ball, Pete would bring it up court. Each time he would reach into his bag of magic. A tricky dribble, followed by a couple of fakes, then the shot. The hesitation step, combined with a behind-the-back dribble. Shots from everywhere.

But Vallely and Bibby were too court-wise to be fooled very often. And when Pete's wizardry did succeed and he swept by the UCLA guards, he still had to contend with Wicks or Rowe. The quick, strong forwards would smoothly drop off the men they were guarding and cover Pete as he came flying toward the basket. And, of course, big Steve Patterson effectively used his height and weight at center.

The finest college team in the nation concentrated its efforts on stopping Maravich, taking its chances that none of his Tiger teammates would get hot. The final score proved the strategy was perfect. As Pete's final statistics showed, not even he could take on a star-studded team and come away victorious. The Bruins' tight defense forced him to commit 18 of LSU's 30 turnovers. And even though he did get open for a number of outside shots, he managed to hit on just 14 of 42 tries from the field. Coach John Wooden's defending national champions swamped the Tigers, 133-84, and held Pete to a low — for him — 38-point performance.

It was a blow to Pete's pride, but he took it with a sense of humor. "I think UCLA should join the NBA," Pete remarked after the game.

Still smarting from the loss to UCLA, the Tigers headed for Honolulu, Hawaii, and the Rainbow Classic tournament. They recovered to defeat St. John's University, 80-70, with Pete pouring in 53 points.

The miracle of Maravich in this contest went far beyond his scoring. It was his total game, an awesome display of basketball which Lou Carnesecca, the St. John's coach, described as: "Unbelievable. On one play he faked a dribble, double-pumped, and hit this guy with a pass off his wrist. Another time I think I saw him bounce the ball between his legs, underneath, to a guy behind him for a layup. He does it all going at full speed. That's what's so amazing."

"Have you ever seen a better college player?" Carnesecca was asked.

The St. John's coach answered the question by describing the Pistol's play in the last 15 minutes of the game. "It was the most electrifying 15 minutes of basketball I've ever seen!"

But the Tigers slumped against Yale, their next opponent, and Pete got into foul trouble early. Although he managed to stay in the game, he wasn't as effective as usual and ended the night with 34 points. LSU lost, 97-94.

One of the opposing players came over to Pete to congratulate him. Pete said, "Thanks, but I'd much rather win. You can have all the points. I'd rather win and play in New York, in the NIT."

"Did you feel tight out there?" asked a fan who had traveled with the team from Baton Rouge. "You know, with Robertson's record and all."

Pete shook his head. "I don't think about the offensive pressures on me. I don't go out there thinking I have to score so many points. But one of these nights," he went on, "everything's going to go in. If I take 40 to 45 shots, I'm going to hit on 40 of 'em. I just know it's coming."

The Tigers' record now stood at seven wins and three losses, a not very awe-inspiring statistic. When Rich Hickman was asked if the team might be winning more if Pete cut down on his fancy passing and dribbling, he defended Pete's style. "When we were freshmen," Hickman recalled, "it was nothing to get bonked in the back of the head by one of Pete's passes. Now that we've learned to anticipate him, his style of play has become routine."

The writer then asked the same question of Joe Dean, a former LSU basketball star. "I think of Pete as the 'White Globetrotter,' " Dean answered. "To most people who read statistics, Pete is regarded chiefly as a scorer, a popgun. But his real appeal, the thing that sets him apart, is his fantastic passing. When he gets to pro ball, where they play one-on-one, he's going to be something to see."

Pete's passing and shooting continued at its fantastic pace. At the same time LSU, with added rebounding help from sophomores Newton and Sanders, was heading toward its best season in many years. After 15 games, LSU showed a 10-5 won-lost record, and Pete's personal scoring pace was a fraction under 47 points a game.

Oscar Robertson's all-time college scoring mark was getting closer. Everybody on the team, and especially Coach Maravich, was rooting for Pete to break the record soon. The tension was growing and affecting the whole team. Press Maravich was especially aware of it. On the night LSU was getting ready to play Ole Miss on the Tigers' court, Press said, "We all want to see him break Robertson's record. Once that's done and out of the way, Pete will be a better basketball player, and we'll all be a lot more relaxed."

The record was well within Pete's reach that

night — and he reached it! He took 46 shots at the enemy basket, connecting on 21 of them. He also collected 11 foul points on 15 tries. His grand total at game's end was 53 points. It was almost incidental that LSU ran away with the game, 109-86.

Oscar Robertson's college scoring record was broken. Pistol Pete had soared past the Big O's three-year total of 2,973 by 14 points. And the huge crowd of 11,856 in LSU's Field House gave Pete a rousing ovation.

The Tigers continued to fight for a place in the NIT. LSU upped its mark to 12 wins and five losses before losing to Alabama, 108-106. It was a hotly contested battle all the way, with Pete narrowly missing the tying goal near the end. Even so, he bucketed 69 points for the evening, the third highest single-game total ever scored in NCAA history.

Pete & Company closed the regular-season campaign by winning their last three games. And with the great finish came the realization of another of the Pistol's dreams — the invitation to the NIT in New York's Madison Square Garden.

The competition was strong but LSU surprised people who didn't give them a chance to get beyond the first preliminary game. With Pete showing the way, the Tigers nipped Georgetown, 83-82. Then LSU moved past Oklahoma, 97-94, and into the semifinals against Marquette. Marquette, however, stuck pins in the LSU bubble, ending the Tigers' tournament dreams with a 101-79 defeat.

Nevertheless, Press' boys had posted a season record of 22 wins and 10 losses. And since some of those defeats had come at the hands of nationally ranked powerhouses, among them UCLA, Kentucky, and Marquette, there was nothing for LSU to be ashamed about.

Pete, of course, had put LSU on the national basketball map. His scoring had fired the Tigers to make the victory column in game after game. And his pro-style play-making had brought out thousands of fans.

Above everything, there was the fame Pete Maravich had brought to LSU. Magazines and newspapers around the country printed his story and the statistics of his matchless varsity career. In the words of one columnist, "The nation hails Pete Maravich of Louisiana State University, college basketball's first point-a-minute career scorer."

The writer noted that Pete had scored 1,381 points in 31 games as a senior, for an average of 44.5. A new all-time single-season average, breaking the one set by Pete, himself, as a junior. Moreover, Pete's three-year total of 3,667 points swept him far past Oscar Robertson's 2,973.

The columnist's final words were, "It's on to the pros for Maravich the Magnificent. No matter which team he plays for, it has to be an improvement over his LSU running mates. Now he'll be among other talented men, who should help bring out the best of his shooting and passing skills."

The Pistol
Enters the Pros

THERE WAS NO DOUBT in anyone's mind that Pete would be among the first players in the 1970 professional draft of college stars. The question was: Would Pete choose the NBA or the ABA? And then, which team would he agree to play for? Sportswriters wanted to know his decision.

"There are so many great teams in pro basketball," he told them, "that it really wouldn't make any difference where I played."

"Come on, Pete," insisted one writer. "The word's been out for weeks that you've been offered big contracts. The highest bids are supposed to be almost two million dollars."

Pete shrugged and answered in his slow southern drawl: "All I know about the pros now is that I've got to put on a few pounds. I weigh about 190, but I'd like to be around 200 or 205."

Pete went on talking about gaining weight while the newspapers, magazines, and television reporters continued their guessing game of how much the pro teams would pay him to play for them.

Then the Carolina Cougars, of the ABA, let it be known they had claimed draft rights to Pistol Pete in a league meeting. The exact amount of money was not made clear, but the Cougars said Pete would be rich if he signed with them.

The reporters asked Press for confirmation of the Cougar offer. The LSU coach also dodged their questions and talked instead about Pete's future as a pro: "I don't think he'll have any adjustment problem. The only adjustment is the one his teammates will have to make to his style of play."

When the elder Maravich was asked, "Will you be going with Pete to whatever team he signs with," Press turned to Pete, standing nearby, and suggested he answer that question. "Dad's staying at LSU," Pete said. "He always wanted to coach me in college and I always wanted him to. We've had our combination. Yes, we've heard all those rumors about a million-dollar father-and-son deal. Been hearing them for two years. But that's just what they are — rumors. We've talked about it and we'd like to cut it off after this year."

So the writers finally had something new to tell their readers.

How, after so many years together, was this going to affect him, Press was asked. "In the last four years we've played to full houses because of Pistol Pete," answered Press. "I'm hoping that interest will stick with these fans we've created. Pistol Pete is a great basketball player, a great showman, and so forth. We're gonna miss him, no question about that."

Baltimore Bullet scout Bob Ferry was asked how he thought Pete would react to the split-up. "He's the only great player I ever heard of with a father for a coach," Ferry said. "I think this has very definitely hurt him emotionally. I think that after being the star of the team for so long, and after playing for his father for so long, he may be starving for discipline. Whenever I see a boy with this many talents, I think of a thoroughbred racehorse, very high strung. I think, against the better competition, the best will come out of him. I just think he's such a great player that he can adjust to anything."

One of the things Pete had already adjusted

to was the idea of being a rich professional basketball player. As a special guest at an LSU dinner, he told the audience: "I just want to take my time about deciding on which league to play in. I want to be sure I'm getting the best deal."

Press, of course, was meanwhile using his knowledge and experience to see that his son got that best deal. After discussing the Cougars' offer, Press revealed that dealings had opened with the NBA's Atlanta Hawks. "The more they told me," Press said, "the more solid Atlanta looked."

When the ABA people heard this, Jim Gardner, owner of the Cougars, assured a reporter the "war" wasn't over. "If we don't get the kid," he said, "we're going to take the money and call on Lou Hudson or Walt Hazzard (two Atlanta stars) — or both of them!" Then he added that the Hawks, "should be more concerned about Hudson and Hazzard than trying to sign some untested, unproven college player."

Gardner, however, was still interested in that "untested, unproven college player." To lure Pete into the ABA, it was reported that Gardner offered a four-year contract for Press to coach the Pittsburgh Pipers of the ABA at a $50,000-a-year salary, and that Pete would have part ownership of the Cougars, and a movie contract.

"When I heard about it," said Pete, "it was

like being in a fairy tale. They were coming back to top Atlanta the way they came back to top the NBA in the bidding for Lew Alcindor [Kareem Abdul-Jabbar]."

Finally, on March 26, 1970, 22-year-old Pete put his signature on a contract. He had chosen the NBA's Hawks, for an estimated 1.8 million dollars to be spread over five years, plus some other benefits. Among those benefits were a new car, a country club membership, and his own apartment in Atlanta.

Pete, Press, and the Hawk management were all delighted. And an NBA official summed up the opinion of the league by saying, "He'll be a bigger draw than Alcindor [Kareem Abdul-Jabbar]. Lew is so good the average fan might tire watching him after a while. Pete's charm lies in the unexpected. The Hawks love to run, and you can bank on Pete getting his share of opportunities to operate as the middle man on three-on-one and three-on-two fast breaks. He'll do it with a flourish that'll bring the fans out of their seats."

But K.C. Jones, a former All-Star guard for the Boston Celtics, doubted Pete would score in the NBA as he had in college. "He scores 50 points," Jones said, "but throws up 100 shots. He's a good shooter, but not a great one."

This wasn't the opinion of former NBA pro

player Jack McMahon: "There's no question in my mind that he can shoot. Anyone who can lead the country in scoring with every defense rigged against him has to be able to shoot."

Pete read all the comments, but his mind was on doing his job for Atlanta. He said, "That [pro basketball] is the one thing I've dreamed of doing and worked for since I was 11 years old. The only thing left for me now is to help win an NBA championship."

The Hawks' coach, Richie Guerin, hoped Pete would do just that. He knew the Pistol would have to adjust to the pro way of play, and that the other Hawks would have to adjust to Pete's style.

"I don't want to change Pete's style to any degree," Guerin said before the 1970-71 NBA season began. "Of course, he can forget about all that scoring. He's going to be more of an asset to us as a passer and playmaker than a scorer. Pete's fancy, sure, but he does things with a purpose. To me, the question is: Can Pete play defense? That's always the toughest adjustment a kid coming from college has to make. Pete is quick enough to be a good defensive player. Quickness and desire is all that's needed on defense. Is he strong enough? Well, if he can keep his weight around 200 pounds, he'll be able to take the beating."

The NBA Rookie

MARAVICH WAS in the pros, and finding it rough. A replay of the first game of the Hawks' season, against the Milwaukee Bucks, went like this:

The Bucks' backcourt star, Oscar Robertson, is guarding Pete tightly. Pete moves the ball to his left and tries to get by, but the Big O seems to have a radar fix on Pete's mind. Robertson matches the Pistol step for step, coming perilously close to slapping the ball loose.

Pete finally gets past the midcourt line. He looks around for someone to pass off to. But his

Atlanta teammates are too tightly guarded. Walt Bellamy, the six-foot-eleven center, is trying to get good position near the basket, and away from seven-foot-four Kareem Abdul-Jabbar. Walt Hazzard, Pete's backcourt partner, is somewhere on the other side of the court. Forwards Lou Hudson and Bill Bridges are weaving around, ducking in and out. Their tactics keep them close to the basket, in rebound position. But they're never clear enough for Pete to risk a pass to either of them. Hazzard, Pete thinks; he should be over here, helping me out.

The 24-second clock shows five seconds left. Get rid of the ball or shoot. Still no Hawk is clear, and Pete has to shoot. Thirty feet from the basket, he launches a desperation shot. It bangs off the rim and into the waiting hands of Jabbar.

Milwaukee comes up and scores. Once again Pete brings the ball upcourt. This time he tries to sweep by the sticky defense of Robertson with a change-of-pace dribble. But as he concentrates on Oscar, another Buck slips up and steals the ball. The crowd's laughter burns the Pistol's ears.

A moment later Pete is watching from the bench, another guard playing the backcourt with Hazzard. And now the Hawks seem to be smoothly, a five-man unit . . .

As Pete sat silently in the Hawk dressing room after the game, the crowd's laughter continued to ring in his mind. So did his mistakes. The passes to teammates that didn't connect. The poor defense. The turnovers when he threw away the ball or had it stolen. The way he tried to play a one-man game and found himself trapped by opponents who could not be fooled.

The rookie was confused. This was the style he had always used. It had succeeded beautifully all through high school and college. The razzle-dazzle dribbling. The better-than-Cousy "blind" passes that tickled the fans and tricked the opposition. All the slick wizardry that had made Pete the prize in the million-dollar battle between the two professional leagues.

Was it that his teammates simply weren't ready for his "show-time" style? Or were they playing to make him look bad?

Pete knew that some of the veterans resented his making so much money, getting so much publicity, and making the starting lineup. Ordinarily a rookie would be expected to work his way in. The resentment had started even before the season had begun. Joe Caldwell, a solid defensive player and rebounder, had told a reporter, "I'm not going to sign a contract for this year unless they pay me at least one dollar more than this rookie!"

The Hawks did offer Caldwell a good contract, but not enough. He jumped to the Carolina Cougars, thereby making good the Cougars' threat to raid the Atlanta team of top players.

Other established Hawks took a "let's wait and see how he does" attitude. Some felt he would have to work hard to earn his salary — and a place in the starting lineup. Walt Hazzard, whose job as number-one guard was threatened by the Pistol, told a sportswriter, "Pete's got to adjust to a new idea. We play the game differently in the pros. He'll learn that the easy way is the best way, and he'll expend less energy than he does now."

But, to Pete's disappointment, not only did he get off to a rocky start, the Hawks also looked terrible as a team. After several very bad defeats, coach Richie Guerin put his annoyance into words. "Maravich has got to discipline himself to the demands of a guard," he said. "He's got a responsibility in that position to do things I want him to and not just dribble around. He's got to work plays."

After the first two months of the season, Atlanta's won-lost record was among the worst in the league. The only NBA teams that had poorer records were Cleveland, Portland, and Buffalo — and they were new, expansion clubs. Pete knew he was part of the reason for the

Hawks' failure. He did some hard thinking about the situation.

"I would lie there on the floor of my room," he wrote later, "staring at the ceiling until three or four in the morning in pure agony. And one of those times I had a heart-to-heart talk with myself. I started thinking about how I had decided, when I was still in grade school, that I was going to become a star in the NBA; about how I had devoted my life since then to basketball; about the thousands of hours I had spent learning to pass the ball behind my back; about how loose and good I had felt until I joined the Hawks. . . ."

The time is February 9, 1971, three months after the disastrous game with Milwaukee. The place: Madison Square Garden. Pete has the ball, bringing it up along the sideline. The Knicks' Walt Frazier glides forward to pressure him. The Pistol switches the ball from right hand to left, then flips it ahead to Walt Hazzard. Hazzard takes the pass, drops it off to Lou Hudson as he goes by, then takes the return pass from Hudson.

As the ball changes hands between Hazzard and Hudson, Maravich moves past Dave DeBusschere. Frazier's contact with Pete is briefly broken. And in that moment, the Pistol is off and darting for the basket. Hazzard's snap pass smacks into his hands and Pete floats in for an easy goal.

The Hawks turn and trot upcourt. Hazzard and Maravich exchange smiles and handslaps as they take their defensive positions.

It was a beautiful demonstration of give-and-go basketball. The kind of playing that demands full cooperation from five players with one purpose in mind.

Something had changed. Not only in the play of Pete Maravich but in the entire Hawks' attitude. Pete scored high. The Hawks had beaten the Knicks. And most important, the Hawks were playing team basketball.

During one series of games in which they won six of eight, an Atlanta sportswriter wrote: "Maravich started doing what nobody does better. Never guilty of lack of hustle and effort, the Pistol used this asset by moving without the basketball. When he got open — and he is impossible to guard because of his quickness — Hazzard hit him with the pass. And except on rare occasions, when he apparently could not resist it, Maravich did not showboat or hog the ball. If the opening no longer existed, he passed to the open man."

The fans weren't laughing any more. And

Atlanta continued to come on stronger, finishing the last month of the regular schedule with 12 victories in 17 games.

Pete — with the rest of the team — had put it all together. His blind passes were working; his teammates had caught his rhythm and were ready for practically anything he threw at them. And he had caught the team's rhythm. His passes were still spectacular, but now they were on target.

Ticking like a clock, the Hawks charged from far back in the Central Division to reach a play-off spot. Even though the Knickerbockers defeated them in the first round, the season proved the Hawks had found themselves. They would be a much stronger team in 1971-72. And part of that strength would come from the "new" Pistol Pete Maravich.

Relaxing after his hectic first season as a professional, Pete talked about it. He admitted his disappointment at receiving only four out of a possible 192 votes for NBA Rookie of the Year. The award had gone to Portland's Geoff Petrie and Boston's Dave Cowens, who had tied for first place. Pete had managed no better than third place in the voting, but he got a strong vote of confidence from Coach Guerin.

"It's a disgrace that Pete Maravich was not

named Rookie of the Year," Guerin said. "Cowens and Petrie are fine players, but neither had a rookie year like Pete. And mark my words, neither will accomplish what Pete will accomplish in this league. There wasn't a better rookie in this league than Pete. I put him in the same class as Oscar Robertson, Jerry West, and Earl Monroe when they came up. You know, it's difficult for a man Pete's age to handle the constant pressure he was exposed to all year. He always impressed me the way he kept his cool through all the criticism and hostility he had to face. To do all that and still have a rookie year like he had, you gotta be some kind of ballplayer."

And you also have to mature as a person. Pete's growing up showed in the honest way he looked back on his rookie year.

"I'd never bothered with defense before," he confessed, "so I certainly learned a lot there. I had to adjust to the other Hawks, just as they had to adjust to me, especially in the area of passing the ball behind the back and all of that. I suppose I learned that there are some moves you can make under the basket in college that you can't make against the bigger and quicker guys in the NBA.

"Now that my first season is over," he said, "I can see how naive I was. I thought I had been through a lot of pressure during my career at LSU — being interviewed by every guy with a pencil, being mobbed and cursed by fans, being triple-teamed at nearly every stop — but that was nothing compared to what happened to me this past season. I've never experienced a year like that in my life, and I hope I never have to go through another one like it. In many ways I feel like I haven't played *one* year in the NBA; I've played *10*. The season ran long for me. I may be the oldest, most experienced sophomore in the history of the game."

Pete had become, in fact, a real pro. Not many NBA players had a better year than the Pistol. He averaged 30 points a game in the last month of the season. He scored 1,880 points in 81 games, for a season average of 23.2, and finished eighth in the NBA scoring race.

The NBA honored the fledgling Hawk by voting him onto its All-Rookie First Team. He had won the distinction the hard way. But the ordeal had made a man of Pete. No longer was he the "cocky kid" whose wisecracks and hair-trigger temper had infuriated fans, referees, and sportswriters.

With his "break-in" year behind him, Pete knew there were many things still to be accomplished. Like being part of an NBA championship team. "I've had the money and the recognition," he said. "Now I want a title."

So did Richie Guerin and the rest of the Hawks. Everyone in Atlanta was looking forward to the coming season. Especially sophomore Pete Maravich, anxious to have the super year that had eluded him in 1971. Certain that his troubles were behind him, Pete assured his fans, "Now I'm ready to play my best!"

A Real Pro

PETE WAS EAGER for the 1971-72 season to begin. When the 1971 training camp opened in September, the Pistol was among the first to arrive. He had gained the 20 pounds he felt he needed to play the grueling 82-game season schedule. Now, at 203 pounds, Pete's six-foot, five-inch frame packed more muscle and he was ready. The stronger guards and heavier forwards wouldn't have an easy time with him this year.

The Atlanta management had shown its confidence in Pete by trading Walt Hazzard. Walt had been Pete's backcourt partner and the team's floor leader of the past season. Hazzard's departure meant that coach Richie Guerin felt Pete was ready to lead the Hawks. As the number-one guard, Pete would direct the team movement and set up the squad each time it went on the attack.

This was what Pete had hoped for, had played for, even when things looked bad the previous year. Here was his chance, and his eagerness to prove he could do it showed in his every move. Under Pete's backcourt direction in the pre-season camp, workout sessions went smoothly. He brought the ball upcourt each time, guiding his teammates into place for set plays. He dribbled in his usual deft way. He passed the ball sharply and accurately. He took return passes and, more often than not, whipped the ball to a teammate in good scoring position. He was the brain that ran the team, and he had learned not to hog the ball. Pete shot when the times were right, but he got the ball to Lou Hudson when the steady-scoring forward was free, or he looped a pass to Walt Bellamy when the big center had worked in close to the basket.

Sportswriters covering the team were impressed by the Hawks' new "quarterback." What impressed them most was Pete's concentration on playing hard-nosed defense. After watching him for the first four days of camp, one writer said, "Pete looks 100 percent better on defense.

He'll do a lot more for this team at *both* ends of the court this year!"

Then suddenly, it seemed, the praise had been too hasty. In the following few days at training camp Pete's play grew ragged and undependable. He missed seeing the open man, and failed to pass off at the right moment. Even worse, he seemed to be uninterested in keeping the ball moving quickly. The other players began complaining that he was loafing. One grumbled, "He must be spending all that money in his mind instead of thinking about where the ball's supposed to go."

It wasn't until the eighth day of practice that the truth came out. Pete told the coach that his throat had been sore for several days and it wouldn't clear up. The trainer took his temperature — the thermometer showed 103 degrees.

The next day Pete's fever wavered between 102 and 103. He could barely eat. Finally a medical examination revealed he was suffering from mononucleosis. The disease was sapping his energy. Training camp continued, but without Pistol Pete.

It was enough to discourage anybody. Pete had weathered the miseries of a rough rookie year, overcome the cutting remarks of hundreds of critics, gone through a mental depression, and come out of it with a healthy attitude. He was ready to do the job in 1971-72. And he had been doing just that when the disease hit him. As his strength waned, his eagerness disappeared, and the gloom of disappointment settled over Pete.

The newspapers jumped on this latest development. The Atlanta *Journal* quoted Pete as saying, "I'll never be back — at least not this year."

The Pistol immediately denied the statement. "What I did say was that I lost 26 pounds in two weeks." He also gave the impression that it would be a long, difficult pull for him to get back into condition to play a whole game. Mononucleosis drains a person of the strength and stamina necessary to do *any* kind of hard work for very long. And Pete, never a husky, tireless performer, was way below his playing weight. Even if he could return to basketball soon, how could he make up for the lost time? The harder he tried, the quicker he would exhaust himself. The quicker he exhausted himself, the longer it would take him to recover his energy to try again.

The Pistol was really discouraged. And he wasn't alone. Both he and Coach Guerin sounded unhappy about Pete's condition when the star guard rejoined the team on November 17, 1971.

"I still have 15 pounds to go," Pete said as the Hawks prepared to meet the Seattle SuperSonics in Atlanta. "I can't play full steam yet. The doctor told me to try but if I got tired to tell the coach to take me out of the game."

And Guerin said, "We expect big things, real big things from Pete. But you must remember that being ill and missing all of the exhibition season and the first 14 games of the regular schedule will be a handicap to him. Maybe it's the kid's fate. Maybe it's the way the ball bounces. But it looks like he has to do everything the hard way."

Pete got in a few minutes of floor-time that night, but he was obviously weak and out of condition. The Hawks had been playing losing basketball without him, and his limited contribution against Seattle indicated things weren't going to get better — unless he did.

Atlanta's fortunes stayed on a bumpy course as the team won some games, lost others. But with each contest Pete played longer, seemed stronger, passed more accurately, and increased his scoring totals. The proof that he had surged all the way back came in a mid-January game against the Philadelphia 76ers.

Pete sparkled from the opening play. His speed and swift change-of-pace dribbles got him through the Philadelphia wall of defense. Hal

Greer couldn't stop him as he shot by for down-the-middle drives to the basket. Billy Cunningham failed to block the bull's-eye jumpers Pete flipped up from near the baselines. When the frustrated 76ers tried to tighten up on Pete, with two men closing in on him as he raced for pay-dirt, the Pistol danced this way and that and out of reach. And when they did succeed in blocking his way, Pete didn't hesitate to rifle smooth passes to free teammates.

In a wild, fantastic orgy of on-the-target shooting, Pete hit the hoop for 18 baskets in 29 attempts, and added 14 of 16 from the foul line. All told, Pete bucketed 50 points, six better than his previous professional high. Pistol Pete also had picked up a number of assists passing off to Lou Hudson, who scored 25 points, and Walt Bellamy, who collected 13. The Hawks defeated Philadelphia, 124-116, and Pete had played the finest all-around game of his life.

The Pistol was grinning like a Halloween pumpkin after the game. So was Richie Guerin, who also expressed surprise that the underweight guard had been able to make it through the whole game. "It was our third game in three nights," the coach said. "He was really tired, and I would have taken him out earlier. But it was close and we needed him in there."

As important as the 50 points were to Pete,

what was even more important were Guerin's words: "We needed him in there."

It was a proud Pete Maravich who told reporters: "I was looking to shoot more than I ever have as a pro. But I want everyone to realize it wasn't for me — it was a team effort. Before the game," he explained, "we got together and decided to express ourselves. We thought we should run more. It worked. Bellamy and the forwards were getting down the court so fast, they were making avenues for me. Our opponents had to adjust and switch off. By the time they did, I had the ball up."

Yes, it was a team effort, Pete emphasized, with full credit to his teammates. This was a different young man from the rookie sportswriters had called "a showoff" and "Shotgun Pete."

Now the Hawks, with Pete as much a playmaker as a scorer, were a threat to every team in the league. Winning basketball was their game, and before long Atlanta had climbed into second place in the Central Division. Not even Milwaukee's Oscar Robertson and Kareem Abdul-Jabbar could stop them in a game played a week after Pete's 50-point performance. In this Hawk victory, Pete scored 35 points and piled up 14 assists.

As if to prove that his 50-point game was no

accident, Pete repeated the total in an Atlanta win over Cleveland at the beginning of February. The point production pleased Pete, but the win pleased him even more.

The Pistol continued playing at a slim 185 pounds (he couldn't gain back the lost 20 pounds), and he was plagued by tendonitis and a bone spur in one toe. It slowed his game a bit, but not enough to stop him from leading Atlanta to a second-place finish behind Baltimore in the Central Division. He did it on scoring. He did it on playmaking. And he did it without sacrificing the razzle-dazzle style that drew the fans.

To the last day of the season, Pete gave every game everything he had. He ran and shot and passed like a demon, pushing himself until he was exhausted and Coach Guerin insisted he rest for a few minutes.

The Hawks were winners and Pete had finally won the respect of the Atlanta writers. Now they were congratulating the Hawk management for signing Pete. One wrote: "Our Pistol's come a long way in two years. He knows what defense is all about, and he plays it. I never thought I'd see the day, but he knows what it means to be a team man. He was underweight, out of shape, mighty unhappy — and still he fought back to make the Hawks a contender."

Other writers pointed out that Pete was under par for many of the 66 games he managed to play as a sophomore, especially the ones when he first rejoined the team. Nevertheless, he scored 1,275 points and averaged 19.3 per game. It was a scoring pace second only to Hudson's, the Hawks' leading point-maker. And Pistol Pete's 393 assists — an average of almost six a game — were tops on the team, even though he missed 16 complete games and portions of others. In fact, noted one columnist, if he had played in enough games to qualify for the NBA assists race, he would have placed 7th in the league. "That," said the writer, "is what a playmaking guard is supposed to do."

With a fine season behind him, Pete outdid himself in the play-offs. In the first round, Atlanta carried the Atlantic Division leaders, the Boston Celtics, to six games before being eliminated. But not because Pete failed in any way. Over those six contests he averaged five rebounds and five assists a game. Moreover, he was Atlanta's ace scorer, totaling 166 points for an average of 27.7 points a game. His closest rival, Hudson, scored 150 points for a 25 points-per-game average.

Pete was an All-Star in that series. In every game, he challenged guard Jo Jo White in one-on-one situations. White, a tough man on defense, couldn't contain Pete. And throughout the series Pete found Lou Hudson with sizzling passes, setting up the Hawk forward for uncontested one-handers all around the basket.

This was the Pete Maravich who, a year earlier, was getting trapped in corners. Who was flinging the ball at teammates who weren't there. Who kept losing the ball because he was still trying to play the way he had in school.

Richie Guerin said it best after the play-offs: "There was a time when Pete could take 40 shots, hit 30 of them, and we'd still get blown off the court. Like I told him — he's not doing us any good if he doesn't get our other players involved in the offense.

"Pete must shoot and pass and defend for us to win. He proved he could do all of it in the play-offs. It's not that I don't want him to score — he hit for 36 and 37 points in two of those games — and when you shoot the way he does, it's important to control the basketball most of the time. But with that kind of freedom comes responsibility, and on this club it's looking for the open man."

What Guerin was saying was that Pete had matured into the leader of the Hawks. He wasn't the complaining kid any more. He had faced his problems and overcome them, winning the respect of the players, writers, and fans. He had become a man.

In every way, the 1971-72 season marked the turning point in the starry career of Pete Maravich. The Pistol had arrived as a superstar of the NBA.

Pete's Future

MANY YEARS HAVE PASSED since 12-year-old Pete rushed into the night, clutching a basketball as if it were a security blanket. That long-ago nightmare is something that Pete can laugh at now. But it took a long time before he could laugh without worrying just a little that something might go wrong.

Pete's early years were filled with problems, more problems than are faced by most kids. He found success too soon, and he had to do all of his growing up in full view of the fans and players and writers. It was the toughest thing he had to do. But by making the grade in the NBA, he showed just how much of a man he really is.

What does the future hold for Peter Press Maravich? Unless bad luck, like a serious physical injury, cuts short his career, he'll be playing pro basketball until he's at least 35. Many great years are still to come.

How many of those years will be championship ones for Pete? That depends on several things. If the Hawks build a well-balanced squad — through smart trades and college draft picks — Atlanta can field a winner. But even with a towering pivot man and solid forwards, the team will go only as far as their star guard takes them. And the Pistol is the kind of player — scorer, playmaker, and team leader — who can take them all the way.

Whatever the future holds for the Hawks, if Pete Maravich continues on his present course he will most certainly achieve his final goal — a place in basketball's Hall of Fame.

Maravich demonstrates his sleight-of-hand magic with a ball.

Pistol Pete at L.S.U. following through in game in which he reached all-time collegiate total score of 2,987 points.

UP